PRAISE FC

You're not alone

◇◇◇◇◇◇◇◇◇◇

"Chelsea's life journey has taken her into places that would be daunting for most of us. Her tenacity and creativity allowed her to turn her extraordinary challenges into a masterful business. She is a guiding force for women everywhere—especially those who need a map. Go where Chelsea leads."

— INDRANI GORADIA, INDRANISLIGHT.ORG

"Chelsea has a wonderful way of sharing her life in order to encourage others that anything is possible—with a little hard work, determination and belief in yourself."

— TRACY TIMM

"One of my favorite quotes by Chelsea was in an article I read about her and it said, 'Many people think that success makes you happy. But, I have found that it's the other way around. Happiness helps people be more successful.' I knew Chelsea and I would be best friends after that. I'm thankful for daily inspiration and for people who bring it to life."

— ASHLEE BROCKGREITENS, SWEETHOMEALOHA.COM

"Chelsea has a way of inspiring people and moving them in the most positive direction. I've been following her for some time now and I'm so grateful our worlds collided. Anything Chelsea touches, I'm there. Including this book. Who wouldn't want more inspiration in their lives?"

— NICOLE PETERS

You're
not
alone

You're not alone

52 Ways to Inspire Change, One Week at a Time

Chelsea Berler

& OTHER INSPIRATIONAL CONTRIBUTORS

YOU'RE NOT ALONE
Copyright © 2015 by Chelsea Berler

Published in Santa Rosa Beach, Florida, USA by Chelsea Berler.
Printed at Cedar Graphics, Inc., Davenport, Iowa, USA.
GetInspiredBook.com

ISBN-10: 069246378X
ISBN-13: 978-0-692-46378-9

AUTHOR CONTACT
Chelsea Berler
5184 Caldwell Mill Rd, Suite 204-102
Birmingham, AL 35244
800-780-8388
hello@getinspiredbook.com

Book cover design and layout by Jill Anderson @ solamaragency.com
Author photograph by Alan Collins, Birmingham, Alabama

First Edition

This book is dedicated to the strong women in my life.

My mother, Debra, and my sisters, Alicia and Jessica.

My daily devotions are always for you. You have made
me stronger than I ever knew I was. Thank you for
your love, your guidance, and your raw honesty.

I love you.

Introduction

◇◇◇◇◇◇◇◇◇◇

"If you don't have anything nice to say, come sit next to me."

— ALICE ROOSEVELT LONGWORTH

"To serve people takes dignity and intelligence. But remember, they are only people with money. And although we serve them, we are not their servants. What we do does not define who we are. What defines us is how well we rise after falling."

— *MAID IN MANHATTAN*

I love both of those quotes from two very different people from very different eras. Yet, both quotes are equally inspiring and entertaining.

Favorite quotations like these started each and every chapter in my first book, *The Curious One*. I've heard so many times that the chosen quotes helped individuals through many a difficult patch and that it inspired them to find the positive in life. That kind of feedback got me thinking about inspiration. I asked myself how I could take those lessons to the next level...and inspire more people to make changes. And at the same time, incorporate the wonderful quotes people cherish and fall back on in times of trouble and need...and when they simply are looking for motivation.

Thus the idea was born for this book.

I turned to good friends and trusted business associates and asked them to provide their favorite quotes and messages that have kept them moving forward day after day. I got so many amazing responses from inspirational contributors that I had enough to fill an entire year with quotes and ways to inspire change, one week at a time.

Things won't change on their own...and to make profound changes takes patience, love, and inspiring words. That's why the profound message in this book is that none of us is alone in this world. It's so much easier to get through each day and make changes for the better with prayer, meditation, and the special inspiring words that have helped other people just like you and me.

During the next year (and hopefully every year after that) as you turn the pages of this book, embrace the words and take them to heart. My sincere hope is that you learn to forgive yourself and forgive others. Embrace any kind of loss, defeat, or hurt as well, because these are the things that have changed us all at the deepest level of your being.

Also notice, as I have, that the chosen quotes are from people of all walks of life and from many periods in history, some real and some fictional. People have selected the words of a wide variety of people from Christopher Robbin to Anne Frank to Ralph Waldo Emerson to Winston Churchill to Pablo Picasso to Douglas Adams (from *The Hitchhiker's Guide to the Galaxy*) to Zig Zigler to Bob Marley and Ferris Bueller. A perfect variety of sources for inspiration and encouragement!

What they all have in common is that these 52 weeks of messages encourage us to "keep going" and have hope that more goodness, success, and hope are on their way. As I read and re-read them, I am constantly pushed in a better direction and motivated. I hope you will be as well.

I know that if you believe in change, there will always be a light at the end of the tunnel. Something better is in store for you and your world.

With this book in your hands, *You're Not Alone!*

With my sincere hope and inspiration,

Chelsea Berler

week

1

Kelly Viall

✧✧✧✧✧✧✧✧✧✧

"Promise me you'll always remember that you're braver than you believe, stronger than you seem, and smarter than you think."

— CHRISTOPHER ROBIN

I think it's important to stop yourself sometimes and realize that the people around you are going through the same things that you are. That you're not alone in worrying about paying the mortgage or about spending enough time with your family versus too much time at work. This is an experience that we're all sharing and we are not alone in that experience.

day
1

day
2

day
3

day
4

day
5

day
6

day
7

week

2

Tina Forsyth

◇◇◇◇◇◇◇◇◇◇

"It doesn't get easier, you get stronger."

— AUTHOR UNKNOWN

Stop looking for the easy path. The so called "secret" for how to achieve success quickly and easily.

Success is not easy—it is earned.

When you are on the path to living your purpose and creating what you want in service to others you WILL be challenged. It will be hard at times. You will have to dig deep. You will want to quit. That's just part of the journey.

Embrace the fact that it can be tough, that it's not for the faint of heart and that EVERY step you take is a reason to celebrate.

day
8

day
9

day
10

day
11

day
12

day
13

day
14

week

3

Sheila Stogol

◇◇◇◇◇◇◇◇◇◇◇

"I don't think of all the misery,
but of the beauty that still remains."

— ANNE FRANK, *THE DIARY OF A YOUNG GIRL*

My mother was a negative person, who looked at the dark side of things, the worst in people, and the most dire outcome. Needless to say, she was not a happy person. I often said she was, "Born to mourn." Instead of perpetuating her gloominess, I learned something valuable: To look away from the darkness...to discover the silver lining and joy in the simplest events. When you're happy, you'll feel great and others will feel better around you. You'll surprise and delight yourself...and attract even more joy and satisfaction.

day
15

day
16

day
17

day
18

day
19

day
20

_____

_____

_____

_____

_____

_____

_____

_____

_____

_____

_____

day
21

week

4

Shawn Shepheard

◇◇◇◇◇◇◇◇◇◇◇

"The best way to predict the future is to create it."

— PETER DRUCKER

Many of us invest little time thinking about the life we want to live.

The key to health and happiness is investing time in getting clear on what you want in all areas of your life, and why you want it.

You can't hit a target that doesn't exist.

Take action everyday to make your dream a reality.

It's the key to being healthy and happy.

day
22

day
23

day
24

day
25

day
26

_____

_____

_____

_____

_____

_____

_____

_____

_____

day
27

day
28

week

5

Dr. Rachna Jain

◇◇◇◇◇◇◇◇◇◇

"All life is an experiment.
The more experiments you make the better."

— RALPH WALDO EMERSON

When you're afraid of doing something, or you're afraid you can't do something, or you're afraid of something you've already done— the biggest thing to remember is that you wouldn't be here if you couldn't handle it. Yes, rejection or failure totally sucks. But you want what you want *only* because it is possible for you to have. And what if things turned out even better than you ever imagined? I like to think of life as being made up of a series of small choices. You only need to make a few good choices to have an amazing life.

day
29

_____

_____

_____

_____

_____

_____

_____

_____

_____

day
30

day
31

day
32

day
33

day
34

day
35

week
6

Kim Bowen

◇◇◇◇◇◇◇◇◇◇◇

"Success is not final, failure is not fatal:
it is the courage to continue that counts."

— WINSTON CHURCHILL

In my life, one of the most shocking discoveries I've made is that the only difference between those who accomplish amazing success and those who wish they could is the courage to try. I always thought some people were just luckier or more blessed than others. Then I took a chance on something when everyone told me to lower my expectations and *bam!* My world tilted and life changed dramatically. Some may be born luckier or more blessed but it is our fear of failing and getting stalled by the "what ifs" that keeps us stuck in mediocrity. I haven't always had the courage to live fearlessly but I can't believe the amazing things that have happened when I did. I no longer want to sit on the sidelines. I want to play big.

day
36

day
37

day
38

day
39

day
40

day
41

day
42

week

7

Gina E. Mallonee

◇◇◇◇◇◇◇◇◇◇◇

"Everything in life is temporary. So if things are going good, enjoy it because it won't last forever. And if things are going bad, don't worry, because it can't last forever either."

— AUTHOR UNKNOWN

Everything is temporary, the good and the bad. This was something I heard from a teacher in high school that really stuck with me. Life and the events that shape us are fleeting. They are moments and nothing more. This thought has pulled me out of the doldrums during the bad times and has me helped to remain grateful during the good times as I continue down my life's journey. I am forced to acknowledge and be thankful that no matter how dark my days may get, there is always hope and light waiting for me just around the corner.

day
43

day
44

day
45

day
46

day
47

day
48

day
49

week

8

Tamara Gold

◇◇◇◇◇◇◇◇◇◇

"The purpose of art is washing the dust of daily life off our souls."

— PABLO PICASSO

Show up for your life. The one you know in your heart. You are meant to live...and magic will happen.

day
50

day
51

day
52

day
53

day
54

day
55

day
56

week
9

Kat Perkins

"Dream it, do it."

— AUTHOR UNKNOWN

I live by the motto "Dream it, do it." You truly can achieve your dreams by working hard, but it is also very important to be kind at the same time. Take time to give back to your community, friends, and family. Be brave, be kind, work hard and "Dream it, do it" will be the motto you live by too!

day
57

day
58

day
59

day
60

day
61

day
62

day
63

week

10

Hillary Rubin

◇◇◇◇◇◇◇◇◇◇◇

"This life is a process of learning."

— LAURYN HILL

Some people call themselves procrastinators when really they have forgotten there are rhythms to life. Perhaps the pause in any creative project, goal, or dream is the very thing you need to learn—what you need to make it even better. Or maybe you as a person need to grow and by giving it space, you can come back to it to see it with fresh eyes.

Allow yourself to have...*space* for things to develop. *Time* for things to develop. And *ease* for things to develop.

Consider being okay with what is, instead of resisting or invalidating yourself.

day
64

day
65

day
66

day
67

day
68

day
69

day
70

_____

_____

_____

_____

_____

_____

_____

_____

_____

_____

week

11

Jeremie Miller

◇◇◇◇◇◇◇◇◇◇

"Don't panic."

— DOUGLAS ADAMS, *THE HITCHHIKER'S GUIDE TO THE GALAXY*

"To provide the security for my family to have amazing adventures together."

This is my "why." The core value statement that drives all of the decisions I make, big and small.

What's your why?

How do your plans today help you achieve your why?

If your plans don't help achieve your why, what can you do instead?

Now, find time today (every day) to do that "instead."

day
71

day
72

day
73

day
74

day
75

_____

_____

_____

_____

_____

_____

_____

_____

_____

day
76

day
77

week

12

Danielle Dekker

◇◇◇◇◇◇◇◇◇◇

"Everybody is a genius. But if you judge a fish by its ability to climb a tree it will live its whole life believing that it is stupid."

— ALBERT EINSTEIN

I am inspired by the contagion of true kindness. It prompts me to infect others. Everyday I desire to put forth a concerted effort to raise the frequency of my surroundings. The seemingly inconsequential act of a smile or holding a door can warm the heart of someone who desperately needed to feel a glimmer of love in the world. Positivity wants to replace negativity. I know, I know...it sounds cliché. It should be simple but I will slip up, probably often. But imagine what could materialize if we practice kindness not to be perfect but to be permanent.

day
78

day
79

day
80

day
81

day
82

day
83

day
84

_____

_____

_____

_____

_____

_____

_____

_____

_____

week

13

Casey Truffo

◇◇◇◇◇◇◇◇◇◇◇

"To feel ambition and to act upon it is to embrace the unique calling of our souls. Not to act upon that ambition is to turn our backs on ourselves and on the reason for our existence."

— STEVEN PRESSFIELD

Do you believe we are spiritual beings having a human experience?

If so, then why do we worry so much about not being perfect—or even good enough? Humans are designed to be imperfect...to make mistakes...to be fallible.

Imagine that you clocked yourself a stiff suit of armor—would you expect your movements really smooth? Would you expect to hit your target every time? Of course not. So let's cut ourselves a little slack when we are in our human experience.

Let's remember who we *really* are. (And...let's forgive ourselves when we forget.)

day
85

day
86

day
87

day
88

day
89

day
90

day
91

week

14

Todd Uterstaedt

◇◇◇◇◇◇◇◇◇◇

"For I know the plans I have for you," declares
the Lord, "plans to prosper you and not to harm
you, plans to give you hope and a future."

— JEREMIAH 29:11

It was about 2 AM and I was tired, cold, and hungry. This was my first time on a real military training exercise near the Demilitarized Zone between North and South Korea. I was the intelligence officer for a combat engineer unit and had no idea what I was doing. The commander radioed me for advice. I was stunned, but responded. He paused and said, "great insight." That was the day I realized a big lesson. Great leaders assume the best in others. His faith in me boosted my confidence. Believe in others and they just might surprise you.

day
92

day
93

day
94

day
95

day
96

day
97

day
98

week

15

William Bradford

◇◇◇◇◇◇◇◇◇◇◇

"Where is the life we have lost in living? Where is
the wisdom we have lost in knowledge? Where is
the knowledge we have lost in information?"

— T.S. ELIOT

1. Be grateful for what you have and work to show it.

2. What you focus on flourishes inside of you.

3. When we fall down it's a chance to take a good look at the ground, think, and act on the opportunity to get up and do better.

4. Be smart, have a plan, and work hard to accomplish your goals.

day
99

day
100

day
101

day
102

day
103

day
104

day
105

week

16

Jessie Haefner

◇◇◇◇◇◇◇◇◇◇

"The strength of a tree lies in its ability to bend."

— AUTHOR UNKNOWN

There have been moments in my life that I thought I was broken. I believed I was what others slung onto me...a poor girl, an unintelligent, useless person taking up space in this world. That image engulfed me. It almost ruined me.

Then there was a moment...a moment when I thought about who I really was, what I was really destined to do in this life. And so it began...a little at first—the glimpse of the rainbow instead of the storm, the optimism of life, the breath, the freedom of living out my true purpose without fear or regret. For today, look into your soul and see yourself for all you are destined to be, for all you are destined to do in this world, and for all that your passion and purpose are destined to change.

day
106

day
107

day
108

day
109

day
110

day
111

day
112

week
17

Corey Whitaker

◇◇◇◇◇◇◇◇◇◇

"Love the life you live. Live the life you love."

— BOB MARLEY

I have heard countless times, "Live each day like it's your last." Every time I hear that I always think about how morbid the idea is. Seriously, how depressing is that? Why not think about every day like it's your *first!* What would you change if that were the case? What relationships would you like to start over? What would you do if you had an entire life ahead of you? Do that. Life is too short to live each day like it's your last.

day
113

_____

_____

_____

_____

_____

_____

_____

_____

_____

_____

day
114

day
115

day
116

day
117

_____

_____

_____

_____

_____

_____

_____

_____

_____

day
118

day
119

_____

_____

_____

_____

_____

_____

_____

_____

_____

_____

week

18

Tracy Bennett Smith

◇◇◇◇◇◇◇◇◇◇

"Be strong, but not rude. Be kind, but not weak. Be bold, but not bully. Be humble, but not timid. Be proud, but not arrogant."

— AUTHOR UNKNOWN

The way we communicate affects everything we do and everyone we interact with. Through that communication we have the choice of making a positive or a negative impact. I try my best to choose positive...every day. It's amazing how a positive, kind attitude and approach towards others can truly make a difference. How we communicate can either be a strength or a weakness so work daily to ensure that yours is a strength.

day
120

_____

_____

_____

_____

_____

_____

_____

_____

_____

_____

day
121

day
122

day
123

day
124

day
125

day
126

week

19

Lisa Bjornson

◇◇◇◇◇◇◇◇◇◇◇

"Every day is a new beginning, take a deep breath and start again."

— AUTHOR UNKNOWN

It sounds so cliché, but each day really is a new day to start over; in fact each moment is. When things don't seem to be going your way, take a deep breath. An actual big, deep breath and then move on. That deep breath can realign you and your thinking, put things into perspective, and calm you down. It puts you in the position to take the next step in your day, preferably towards a happier you!

day
127

day
128

day
129

day
130

day
131

day
132

day
133

week

20

Tracey Ingle

◇◇◇◇◇◇◇◇◇

"And then the day came when the risk to remain tight in a
bud was more painful than the risk it took to blossom."

— ANAÏS NIN

God never gives us a burden we cannot carry. Ever. The problem is in asking, "Why?" We assume there is a meaning for us. Sometimes the lesson is for us, but sometimes the lesson is for someone else, a witness to our struggle. We are asked to carry the burden simply because we can. But the reason the "Why" exists is for the witness. Knowing this, I no longer need to understand every hurdle put in my path. And you can't even imagine the energy I regained by not constantly seeking an answer to "Why?"

day
134

day
135

day
136

day
137

day
138

day
139

day
140

week

21

Jane Mell Balek

◇◇◇◇◇◇◇◇◇◇

"...never take counsel of your fears."

— GENERAL GEORGE S. PATTON

Never underestimate the power of a warm smile and a kind word. We can't know everyone's struggle or story, but a warm gesture may turn out to be the very thing that changes someone's day.

day
141

day
142

day
143

day
144

day
145

day
146

day
147

week

22

Melissa Wilson

◇◇◇◇◇◇◇◇◇◇◇

"Travel is fatal to prejudice, bigotry, and narrow-mindedness."

— MARK TWAIN

I am not normally a witty-quote-of-my-own kind of girl but throughout my 42 years on this earth I have learned a few things I am happy to share. I believe that with kindness anything can be accomplished. If you ask or are asked to do the most horrible or menial of all tasks with kindness and purpose you are more likely to follow through. I believe that you are only as good as your leader. If you have a terrible leader you must find it in you to make your own path as it is hard to succeed if you don't have a good leader to pave the path. Last, I believe that new beginnings are always an option. It's never too late to start over. Don't ever feel like you are stuck, especially in what you do to make a living. You have a choice everyday. You can make a different choice and can take a different path if you chose. So choose wisely and always do what makes you happy. I believe everyone has greatness, so find your greatness and be extraordinary.

day
148

day
149

day
150

day
151

day
152

day
153

day
154

week
23

D. Alex Tino

✧✧✧✧✧✧✧✧✧✧

"That's why I began doing makeup in the first place:
I was hoping that through helping people see the beauty
in themselves, I could try and find it in me."

— KEVYN AUCOIN

My advice to anyone is to look in your mirror and accept that you are here for a reason and you are beautiful...and if anyone tells you any different, then screw them!

day
155

day
156

day
157

day
158

day
159

day
160

day
161

week
24

Erin Ferree Stratton

◇◇◇◇◇◇◇◇◇◇

"I am not a glutton—I am an explorer of food."

— ERMA BOMBECK

Seek adventure. Find a thing you've never seen, eat foods you've never tasted, and make something you've never tried to make. Ask a friend to teach you something they are passionate about. Do something out of character on purpose. Choose simple ways to expand the borders of your life a bit every day, and discover the richness that lies just beyond what you're used to.

day
162

day
163

day
164

day
165

day
166

day
167

day
168

week
25

Amy Bryan Baggett

◇◇◇◇◇◇◇◇◇◇

"Life moves pretty fast. If you don't stop and look
around once in a while, you could miss it."

— FERRIS BUELLER

As a working mom with two small children, I find there is never enough time during the day to finish all of my tasks. However, instead of dwelling on what I *didn't* finish on any given day, I try to focus on what I *did* complete...what I *did* accomplish...and hopefully, the fun I had along the way.

day
169

day
170

day
171

day
172

day
173

day
174

day
175

week
26

Ben Kaplan

◇◇◇◇◇◇◇◇◇◇◇

"One of the sanest, surest, and most generous joys of life comes from being happy over the good fortune of others."

— ROBERT A. HEINLEIN

True wealth can be measured not in your pocket, but in the richness of your relationships. Gratitude for all those around you is immeasurably rewarding.

day
176

day
177

day
178

day
179

day
180

day
181

day
182

week
27

Meghan Ziegs

◇◇◇◇◇◇◇◇◇◇

"Let us run with perseverance the race that is set before us."

— HEBREWS 12:1

Never let anyone tell you that *you can't*. My greatest and most treasured achievements have been things that I was told I could never do due to my location, gender, bank account, and personality. I now make it my goal to prove them all wrong and I do it *for me*. I can and I will—just watch me!

day
183

day
184

day
185

day
186

day
187

day
188

day
189

week

28

Chanel Abislaiman

<>

"He's not perfect. You aren't either, and the two of you will never be perfect. But if he can make you laugh at least once, causes you to think twice, and if he admits to being human and making mistakes, hold onto him and give him the most you can. He isn't going to quote poetry, he's not thinking about you every moment, but he will give you a part of him that he knows you could break. Don't hurt him, don't change him, and don't expect for more than he can give. Don't analyze. Smile when he makes you happy, yell when he makes you mad, and miss him when he's not there. Love hard when there is love to be had. Because perfect guys don't exist, but there's always one guy that is perfect for you."

— BOB MARLEY

Relationships require constant nurturing, attention and communication with the ability to adapt to change frequently.

The only true constant throughout your life journey together is what brought you together in the first place—love.

Love passionately. Live fully. Give selflessly.

day
190

day
191

day
192

day
193

day
194

day
195

day
196

week
29

Stacy Perkins

◇◇◇◇◇◇◇◇◇◇

"Whatever He puts in front of you,
do it with Great Love,
this is what makes
any day
anybody
any life
great!"

— ANN VOSKAMP

Life can get so hectic. We can easily get lost in today's to-do's that we lose sight of what matters or who matters most...loving each other. Today is a new day, a new start and a gift from God. It's not about getting every task complete. It's about...Who did I love today? How did I love today? When we give of ourselves it fills our heart in so many unexpected ways. Where can you 'be' love in your life today?

day
197

day
198

day
199

day
200

day
201

day
202

day
203

week

30

Ashlee Brockgreitens

◇◇◇◇◇◇◇◇◇◇

"Never interrupt someone doing what you said couldn't be done."

— AMELIA EARHART

Traveling into the unknown is something that can be scary, but following your heart in all areas of life is what we are all destined to do. Amelia Earhart is someone that did what she wanted, regardless of fear or belief in ability, and in return, she saw the world while proving everyone wrong. The combination of courage and being told what you can or cannot do is what dreams are made of, regardless of where you may end up. Your goals in life should be limitless, otherwise you aren't dreaming big enough.

day
204

day
205

day
206

day
207

day
208

day
209

day
210

week
31

Lauren Bates

◇◇◇◇◇◇◇◇◇◇◇

"Live every day with intention."

— MARY ANNE RADMACHER

Today, look at yourself in the mirror. Say these words: Life can be hard, but I will always strive to be better. I will love deeply and never regret. I will be strong and courageous. I will always believe in myself. Today I will overcome.

day
211

day
212

day
213

day
214

day
215

_____

_____

_____

_____

_____

_____

_____

_____

_____

day
216

day
217

week
32

Paul Sigafus

◇◇◇◇◇◇◇◇◇◇

"A master in the art of living draws no sharp distinction between his work and his play, his labor and his leisure, his mind and his body, his education and his recreation. He hardly knows which is which. He simply pursues his vision of excellence through whatever he is doing and leaves others to determine whether he is working or playing. To himself, he always seems to be doing both. Enough for him that he does it well."

— LAWRENCE PEARSALL JACKS

No one wants to sleepwalk through their own life. Part of each of us wants to be fully awake to the possibilities within and around us, whatever the circumstances of our lives. As we awaken and respond to our own divinely given vision of excellence, we are freed from both ego and fear, and in each area of our lives we become fully alive. What vision of excellence beckons to you? Life fully lived is waiting for you.

day
218

day
219

day
220

day
221

day
222

day
223

day
224

week

33

Lisa Canfield

◇◇◇◇◇◇◇◇◇◇

"If you're going to tell people the truth, you'd better make them laugh; otherwise they'll kill you."

— GEORGE BERNARD SHAW

There are very few things in this world that can't be made at least a little better by laughing until you pee your pants.

day
225

day
226

day
227

day
228

day
229

day
230

day
231

week
34

R. Justin Bing

✧✧✧✧✧✧✧✧✧✧

"Find out who you are—and do it on purpose."

— DOLLY PARTON

Growing up I always had a sense that I was "different" in some ways than other children. I never really fit in with your average schoolyard clicks. And for so many years I thought this was a negative thing, something wrong with me. But what I now know is that being different is what defines my creativity and my distinct place in this world. I've come to not only embrace the qualities that make me unique but love myself because of them. I know who I am and what I have to offer and it's rooted in the things that set me apart from my peers.

day
232

day
233

day
234

day
235

day
236

day
237

day
238

week
35

Indrani Goradia

◇◇◇◇◇◇◇◇◇◇◇

"It is easier to build strong children than to repair broken men."

— FREDERICK DOUGLASS

Our lives have become so very crowded and loud and chaotic. We sometimes feel that we are out of control. I have found that silence is the only way to listen to my deepest desires. The "should" voices are often so loud that I have to just leave the crazy and just be with silence. I have found ways to enter silence even when I am in a crowd and that has been my way to solace.

Our silence provides shelter for the homeless parts within each of us. Shelter and sanctuary are necessary to move up the evolutionary ladder to our essential selves. So when you want to speak, find an ear to provide sanctuary and when you feel lost, find a time for silence so you may provide shelter for yourself from your internal storms.

day
239

day
240

day
241

day
242

day
243

day
244

day
245

week

36

Kay White

◇◇◇◇◇◇◇◇◇◇

"Words have the power to both destroy and heal.
When words are both true and kind they can change our world."

— AUTHOR UNKNOWN

It's so easy to just go on to default isn't it? Day-to-day, saying the same old things, responding in the same old way.

Stop. Think. Decide how you want to respond or come across by considering your words.

Silence is underestimated. Taking time to pause is underestimated. Do both more. Choose if or how you want to respond. Everyone wants to be heard and understood.

What's interesting is it's easier to be heard and understood when you take the time to listen to and understand other people first. At home, with friends, at work—everywhere in fact.

day
246

day
247

day
248

day
249

day
250

day
251

day
252

week
37

Angela Marino

◇◇◇◇◇◇◇◇◇◇

"Being deeply loved by someone gives you strength,
while loving someone deeply gives you courage."

— LAO TZU

Strength: A good or beneficial quality or attribute of a person or thing.

Love is going to knock you down more than once with the painful blows it delivers from time to time. It hurts. It hurts so deeply. You will close yourself off and want to run from the pain. Don't. Soak it in. Feel it in your gut and down to your innermost soul. Then let it hurt more. Cry, scream and ask the question, "Why me?' Your strength will be born time and time again, and become stronger with each and every blow. Don't become discouraged. Allow your heart to remain open, because you see, this pain, it can also be amazingly beautiful and pure. All of the intricate, delicate and sensitive parts of your hidden self will begin to flourish and flourish freely.

Don't feel ashamed for feeling weak or helpless. From this pain and weakness you will gain your greatest strength. The strength of loving yourself for who you are, not what someone else wants you to be. It is from this pain that you will learn who you want to be. It is from this pain that you will find it deep within yourself to become what you have always wanted to be. You. Perfectly and beautifully, you.

day
253

day
254

day
255

day
256

day
257

day
258

day
259

week

38

Tina Hofer Medico

◇◇◇◇◇◇◇◇◇◇

"And above all, watch with glittering eyes the whole world around you because the greatest secrets are always hidden in the most unlikely places. Those who don't believe in magic will never find it."

— ROALD DAHL

There is magic just below the surface of each passing day. Realities and responsibilities may fog up your lenses and prevent you from seeing it, but it's there. The lighthearted joy. The curious wonder. Limitless possibilities for your future. The fullness of a day spent in nature or with the people you love. It's all there just waiting for you to find your way back.

If there's one thing I know for sure, it's that you can always find your way back to that place through the simple act of *play*. Color on the sidewalk. Climb a tree. Write a story. Use your imagination. Run for the simple pleasure of moving your body through the world. Ride a razor scooter. Throw a costume party. Draw. Paint. Dream wildly. Play with abandon. Then look up and with fresh eyes see the world anew—full of light, possibility, love and magic.

day
260

day
261

day
262

day
263

day
264

day
265

day
266

week

39

Mark Groves

◇◇◇◇◇◇◇◇◇◇

"Do the best you can until you know better.
Then when you know better, do better."

— MAYA ANGELOU

Our lives are composed of moments. Moments that come and go, fleeting just like the thoughts that go with them. Today, focus on each and every moment. It is from that space that we can start to see that it only takes a moment to shift our lives and the lives of others. We have mere moments to decide the words we speak and how we want those words to impact the world. The moments of today will have a rippling effect on what tomorrow will look like for not only yourself, but all of the people whose lives you touch today. You actually have the ability to shift the world with a whisper. What are you whispering?

day
267

day
268

day
269

day
270

day
271

day
272

day
273

week
40

Stacie Kenton

◇◇◇◇◇◇◇◇◇◇◇

"The day will be what you make it, so rise, like the sun, and burn."

— WILLIAM C. HANNAN

Let today be the start of something new.

Forge your own trail. Go your own way. Set forth on your next big adventure.

And wherever you go, go with all your heart.

day
274

day
275

day
276

day
277

day
278

day
279

day
280

week

41

Jodi Hume

◇◇◇◇◇◇◇◇◇◇

"We only live once, but if we play our
cards right…once is enough."

— JOE LEWIS

It was cold and raining and my two-year-old was begging to go outside. After several rounds of "Why?" I snapped, "Because I said *no!*" in hopes to end it. But instead, his eyes lit up with pure delight: "Then just say *yes* mommy!"

Momentarily stunned, I felt the simple logic of a toddler dissolve my objections with the gravitational pull of what matters most. 40-minutes and several mud pies later, my freezing fingers were forgotten as we knelt cheek to cheek, marveling at a giant spider web shimmering in the mist.

I almost missed out on playing my cards well that day. How will you play yours today?

day
281

day
282

day
283

day
284

day
285

day
286

day
287

week
42

Mike Flannery

◇◇◇◇◇◇◇◇◇◇

"All truth passes through three stages. First,
it is ridiculed. Second, it is violently opposed.
Third, it is accepted as being self-evident."

— ARTHUR SCHOPENHAUER

It can be difficult and scary to stand alone for your truth, but in the end the rewards are worth the effort.

day
288

day
289

day
290

day
291

day
292

day
293

day
294

week
43

Katie Hellmuth Martin

◇◇◇◇◇◇◇◇◇◇◇

"Honesty, like sanity, is the best policy."

— KATIE HELLMUTH MARTIN

Morning is the first ray of fresh hope. When you awaken with the first morning bird, your body is fresh from yesterday's input, and you are free to begin again.

Mornings are your first touch of freedom in your day where you are alone to set up how the day may go. Two factors go into having a great day: 1. Knowing that your day may take a sharp turn to a place you never imagined. 2. Sleeping the night before. You release the day in the evening, and go to bed with a book or magazine in print, not a lit device, so that your brain can absorb natural sleep hormones that smother you in peace.

day
295

day
296

day
297

day
298

day
299

day
300

day
301

week

44

Elisa Hallerman

◇◇◇◇◇◇◇◇◇◇

"Our Greatest Fear—
it is our light not our darkness that most frightens us
Our deepest fear is not that we are inadequate.
Our deepest fear is that we are powerful beyond measure.
It is our light not our darkness that most frightens us.
We ask ourselves, who am I to be brilliant,
gorgeous, talented and fabulous?

Actually, who are you not to be?
You are a child of God.
Your playing small does not serve the world.

There's nothing enlightened about shrinking so that
other people won't feel insecure around you.

We were born to make manifest the glory of
God that is within us.

It's not just in some of us; it's in everyone.
And as we let our own light shine,
we unconsciously give other people
permission to do the same.

As we are liberated from our own fear,
Our presence automatically liberates others."

— MARIANNE WILLIAMSON

day
302

day
303

day
304

day
305

day
306

day
307

day
308

week
45

Kelly Perkins Robinson

◇◇◇◇◇◇◇◇◇◇

"Courage is not the absence of fear, but rather the judgement that something else is more important than fear."

— AMBROSE REDMOON

I was lucky enough to grow up in a small Midwest town near most of my family. Through the years and as I get older, I've come to realize that there is nothing more important than family and our legacy. My life goal is to instill the importance of family in my own children, so that someday, they too will place the same value on family and continue the tradition. Without family, we are nothing.

day
309

day
310

day
311

day
312

day
313

day
314

day
315

week
46

Amanda McNelly-Goldberg

◇◇◇◇◇◇◇◇◇◇

"Come hell or high water, you can and will and you are not alone."

— BOB MCNELLY

(WISE WORDS FROM MY DAD)

Being the best mother, wife, sister, daughter and friend you can be while holding on to some sense of who *you* are in the mix is a huge undertaking. When you attempt to balance everything on your own frustration can quickly ensue. I try to remember to lean on those I love for support and encouragement. It's always refreshing to know I don't have to go at it alone. Plus it makes this journey of life way more fun!

day
316

day
317

day
318

day
319

day
320

day
321

day
322

week
47

Sabina Hitchen

◇◇◇◇◇◇◇◇◇◇

"Life is not a dress rehearsal."

— AUTHOR UNKNOWN

You are Powerful.

Repeat after me: I am powerful. How does it feel to say those words? What does it mean to you? Do you believe in your power? For years I felt like a fraud saying those words because I didn't understand them. I thought that power was something external. Something that could only be unlocked when I was financially successful, and something I confused with being popular. Many of us feel we have to exert external force to get what we want out of work and life. But the truth is, feeling powerful in your own life is already within reach. It's already within *you*. It's there, patiently waiting for you to tap into it. Where does it come from? It comes when you live as your authentic, true self freely and fearlessly (or despite of fear). It presents itself when you share your unique gifts with others who are waiting for them right now, as we speak. You will feel it pulse through your body when you face down your discomfort zone, and keep moving forward even when experiences feel new, unknown and uncomfortable. Your power will bubble up to the surface when you go against your desire to move fast and be "more," and instead slow down and be still, listening to the guiding wisdom within you that is your soul's voice. Want to feel powerful? Want to be powerful? You already are, my friend. The power is already within you, and it has been all along...now go get it!

day
323

day
324

day
325

day
326

day
327

day
328

day
329

week

48

Andrea J. Lee

◇◇◇◇◇◇◇◇◇◇◇

"To move forward, we have to leave something behind."

— *INTERSTELLAR*

Every action has an equal and opposite reaction, says Newton's Third Law of Motion. In outer space, this means that to move forward, sometimes you have to throw something big behind you at high speeds. The speed at which you go depends on how much stuff you throw, and how firmly you throw it.

I'm discovering that this same law applies to living. To go forward well, I have to be willing to let go of old things. It might even mean giving up hope of ever having a better past. Every time I'm ready for a new adventure, I've learned to celebrate, then say goodbye to former versions of me.

day
330

day
331

day
332

day
333

day
334

day
335

day
336

week
49

Irwin J. Lee

◇◇◇◇◇◇◇◇◇◇◇

"Don't take life too seriously. You'll never get out of it alive."

— ELBERT HUBBARD

Hard times will come. When they do, remember: keep your chin up, take it one day at a time, know who loves you, and never, never give up.

day
337

day
338

day
339

day
340

day
341

day
342

day
343

week
50

Heather Lynn Ludwick

◇◇◇◇◇◇◇◇◇◇

"Everyone you meet is fighting a battle you
know nothing about. Be kind. Always."

— AUTHOR UNKNOWN

All of us have struggles, all of us have demons and until you have walked a mile in that other person's shoes, please don't judge them. Have you ever caught yourself looking at someone attractive who just walked into the room, or even more destructive watched someone very unattractive walk in and think negative thoughts? I work every day not to judge, sometimes subconsciously I fail. I have spent my entire life being judged for one thing or another, as have most of us. There are times the judgement has been good, there have been times the judgment has been harsh. Nonetheless, whether others liked or didn't like me, I would wake up every day, go to work and try and make a positive difference in the children and adults I work with. I truly believe every one of us are fighting our own battles and are truly good inside. The judgement from others is what makes us feel differently about this world and those around us. It is important to not judge ourselves and to teach our young not to judge because it only spreads hate. Be a role model, love one another and teach love.

day
344

day
345

day
346

day
347

day
348

day
349

day
350

week

51

Amy Dier

◇◇◇◇◇◇◇◇◇◇

"Owning our story can be hard but not nearly as difficult
as spending our lives running from it. Embracing our
vulnerabilities is risky but not nearly as dangerous as giving up
on love and belonging and joy—the experiences that make us
the most vulnerable. Only when we are brave enough to explore
the darkness will we discover the infinite power of our light."

— BRENÉ BROWN

I have experienced trauma, loss, sorrow, happiness, joy, and tender moments. All of these experiences are a part of me and have made me who I am. Because of the magic of love, the trauma in my life does not define me any longer and has moved through me like a river. There are still moments of grief, but I welcome my feelings and choose to keep living the human experience. Whatever *your* story is, *you* can choose to love.

day
351

day
352

day
353

day
354

day
355

day
356

day
357

week

52

Amber LaFramboise

◇◇◇◇◇◇◇◇◇◇◇

"What's right is what's left if you do everything else wrong."

— ROBIN WILLIAMS

The raw truth is that at times I'm incredibly insecure, insensitive, and completely unsure. I say the wrong thing, I make hasty decisions, and I'm certain that I have offended hundreds of people, possibly more. I get frustrated when I should be patient and I swear more than I should.

Thankfully, I'm surrounded by a world of gloriously imperfect people who are just as unsure, unintentional, and completely vulnerable as I am!

The "inspiration" I can offer is the sweet truth that we all get to choose to wholeheartedly hug our imperfections and say, "Yep, sounds like me." Say it often and say it boldly. Own that shit.

day
358

day
359

day
360

day
361

day
362

_____

_____

_____

_____

_____

_____

_____

_____

_____

day
363

day
364

day
365

Bonuses

◇◇◇◇◇◇◇◇◇◇◇

Sorry, I couldn't stop at just 52!
Here are a few bonuses that I love too!

Kari Jo Petrick Harris

◇◇◇◇◇◇◇◇◇◇◇

"90% of success is between the ears. Don't let anyone rob you today of your positive mindset. Protect it today at all costs. And let's make a difference."

— AUTHOR UNKNOWN

Each year I am grateful...to celebrate another birthday, another year with my husband, another year to be a mom, another day to *live*.

And now as I enter my 40's, I have reached a peaceful, calm in my life. Which sounds crazy because my husband is a coach, I have 2 jobs (which I love by the way) and 5 beautiful girls. So it seems life should become full of chaos—and don't get me wrong sometimes it is—but it's our chaos and life is so good. We are truly blessed.

Each day I make a promise to my myself...to really live. Because what you say to yourself will take you where you want to go.

You can make a difference. Having a positive attitude does matter. And yes—you and I—we can make a difference in this world.

Go to bed each night...thankful, forgiving, with no regrets.

If you fall, no worries, get up. If you make a mistake, no worries, try again. If you are tired, perfect, you've given your best. Rest.

Be kind. Be grateful. Be you.

Danielle Doby

◇◇◇◇◇◇◇◇◇◇

"You are what you love. Not what loves you back."

— @IAMHERTRIBE

I always say to never stop being too much. Never stop loving too much, caring too much, saying too much. Your words, your story, you sharing your journey with those around you has the possibility to mold and move mountains. It holds the power to change lives, unite hearts and crack open worlds. You never know where your words could lead you, who it could lead and connect you to, or who you could help heal by your vulnerability in sharing your life's path. Your story matters, you matter, and I hope you will always hold that close.

Jill Anderson

◇◇◇◇◇◇◇◇◇◇

"If you keep your destiny in mind, every moment in life becomes an opportunity for moving closer to it."

— ARTHUR GOLDEN

Believe in the power of intention. Put out there into the world what you most desire in life. Speak it into existence.

Chelsea Berler

◇◇◇◇◇◇◇◇◇◇

"If the only prayer you ever say in your entire
life is thank you, it will be enough."

— MEISTER ECKHART

Connect with Chelsea

◇◇◇◇◇◇◇◇◇◇◇◇◇

On the Web

- mostlychelsea.com
- solamaragency.com

Social Media

- twitter.com/chelseaberler
- facebook.com/mostlychelsea
- pInterest.com/mostlychelsea
- instagram.com/mostlychelsea

For Speaking Opportunitites

- hello@getinspiredbook.com
- 800.780.8388

Keep in Touch

- getinspiredbook.com
- facebook.com/thecuriousbook